BOXING FOR BOYS

BOXING
FOR BOYS

BY

REGTL. SERGT.-MAJOR E. B. DENT

Army Gymnastic Staff

Instructor in Boxing at the Army Headquarters Gymnasium, Aldershot

The Naval & Military Press Ltd

Published by

The Naval & Military Press Ltd
Unit 5 Riverside, Brambleside
Bellbrook Industrial Estate
Uckfield, East Sussex
TN22 1QQ England

Tel: +44 (0)1825 749494

www.naval-military-press.com
www.nmarchive.com

*In reprinting in facsimile from the original, any imperfections are inevitably reproduced
and the quality may fall short of modern type and cartographic standards.*

PREFACE

NEVER before has the value of boxing as an aid to developing character in boys been so widely recognized as now. As a means of training a boy to use his brains, eyesight, and muscles in unison, imbuing him with the best sporting interests and encouraging chivalry, boxing is, I consider, unequalled.

In the hope that my long experience in teaching boxing may be of use to others, I have compiled this book. It will help those who wish to teach boys; it will enable a father to train his sons; or it will enable a boy to master the elements of the science unaided.

E. B. DENT, R.S.M.,
Army Gymnastic Staff.

HEADQUARTERS GYMNASIUM,
ALDERSHOT.

FOREWORD

THE ever increasing popularity of boxing is principally due to the fact that it is being more and more widely appreciated for its beneficial influence in building up the character of those who practise it for the love of the sport. It is, in the first place, a manly and healthful exercise, and if it is taught and followed in its true spirit it develops tenacity, magnanimity, fortitude and courage. It teaches the novice to "play the game," to be generous to a weaker opponent, to accept defeat in good part, and to bear pain with a smile. Its beneficial physical effect is well established, so, as an exercise for boys, it is, beyond all doubt, excellent, while its moral influence is of the best. Boxing, systematically taught to the youth of the nation, will have a marked elevating influence on the national character.

CONTENTS

	PAGE
INTRODUCTORY	1
WHEN TO START	3
KIT	3
PLAY-ROOM	4
ON GUARD	4
SPARRING, OR "ON GUARD," WITH ACTION OF THE ARMS	5
THE ADVANCE	5
THE RETIRE	6
MOVING TO THE LEFT AND RIGHT	6
TURNING	6
SWAYING	7
THE CLENCHED FIST	7
STEPPING IN	7
THE "POINT" AND "MARK"	8
THE LEFT LEAD	8
RIGHT HAND GUARD FOR POINT	9
RIGHT HAND GUARD FOR MARK	9
LEFT HAND GUARD FOR MARK	9
LEFT FOREARM GUARD	9
RIGHT FOREARM GUARD	9
RIGHT AT POINT	10
LEFT AT MARK	10
RIGHT AT MARK	10
FEINTING	11
DUCKING	11
DUCK TO RIGHT AND COUNTER WITH LEFT AT POINT	12
DUCK TO RIGHT AND COUNTER WITH LEFT AT MARK	12
DUCK TO RIGHT AND LEFT HAND UPPERCUT	13
GUARD FOR UPPERCUT	13
DUCK TO LEFT AND RIGHT HAND CROSS-COUNTER	13
DUCK TO LEFT AND RIGHT HAND COUNTER AT POINT	14
DUCK TO LEFT AND RIGHT HAND COUNTER AT MARK	14
DUCK TO LEFT AND RIGHT HAND UPPERCUT	15

CONTENTS

	PAGE
SLIPPING	15
THE SIDE-STEP	16
HOOK HITS, LEFT AT HEAD OR BODY	16
RIGHT HOOK AT HEAD OR BODY	17
DEVIATING, OR PUTTING A BLOW ASIDE	17
BLOCKING	18
IN-FIGHTING	19
SKIPPING	25
MEDICINE BAG	26
LESSON I.—FOOTWORK	30
LESSON II.—LEADING AND GUARDING	34
LESSON III.—LEADING AND COUNTERING	37
LESSON IV.—FEINTS	42
LESSON V.—DUCKING RIGHT AND COUNTERING WITH LEFT	48
LESSON VI.—DUCKING LEFT AND COUNTERING WITH RIGHT	52
LESSON VII.—SLIPPING AND COUNTERING WITH LEFT	56
LESSON VIII.—SIDE-STEP, FOREARM GUARD, HOOK HITS, DEVIATING, BLOCKING	59
NOTES ON CONDUCTING "LOOSE PLAY"	62

LIST OF PLATES

	PAGE
CLASS OPENED OUT FOR LEG-WORK	21
CORRECT POSITION FOR OFFENCE AND DEFENCE ...	22
MEDICINE BAG—FIRST PRACTICE	27
MEDICINE BAG—THIRD PRACTICE	28
LESSON I.—PRACTICE 1	31
ON GUARD: CORRECT AND INCORRECT	32
LESSON II.—PRACTICES 1 AND 3	35
LESSON III.—PRACTICE 1	36
LESSON III.—PRACTICE 2	39
LESSON III.—PRACTICE 3	40
LESSON IV.—PRACTICE 1	43
LESSON IV.—PRACTICE 2	44
LESSON IV.—PRACTICE 3	45
LESSON IV.—PRACTICE 4	46
LESSON V.—PRACTICES 1 AND 2	49
LESSON V.—PRACTICES 3 AND 4	50
LESSON VI.—PRACTICES 1 AND 2	53
LESSON VI.—PRACTICES 3 AND 4	54
LESSON VII.—PRACTICES 1, 2, AND 3	57
LESSON VIII.—PRACTICES 1, 2, AND 3	58
LESSON VIII.—PRACTICE 4	60
"IN-FIGHTING"	63
REGTL. SERGT.-MAJOR E. B. DENT	64

BOXING FOR BOYS

INTRODUCTORY.

My system of boxing instruction has proved eminently successful during the twenty-one years I have been teaching on the Army Gymnastic Staff at Aldershot and elsewhere. During that period I have had a wide experience in instructing officers and other ranks, public school boys, Boy Scouts, Church Lads' Brigades, and boys attending private schools, besides my own family. My unique experience I now embody in this book.

Boxing Instructors of clubs or schools frequently get very large classes, and in such cases it is impossible to give individual instruction. I have devised a method by which this can be overcome without detriment to the backward or shy pupil, who otherwise would get little or no tuition.

In such cases the best way to proceed is for

the Instructor or Master, at the first lesson, to pick out those boys who show most promise, and make them leaders, as would be done in a physical training class. Give each leader a pupil. Then call the whole class inwards, and thoroughly explain what each leader and pupil has to do. The Instructor should then walk round the class, giving each leader a turn as pupil. In this way the practical points of the lesson are clearly demonstrated both to the leaders and pupils.

The Instructor should always open instruction with a few minutes' leg-work, medicine ball, or skipping in class, as an introductory exercise to the lesson to be taken.

When the class has mastered the lessons, and has reached a good standard of proficiency, the leaders should present their pupils to the Instructor for passing out. This examination should entitle those boys who have been giving instruction to be graded as leaders. The pupils who pass the test should, in turn, be encouraged to take the position of leaders, and so qualify in time. Badges could be given to those who qualify as leaders. This method will be found most successful with Boy Scouts and in schools.

WHEN TO START.

I have often been asked at what age a boy should start boxing. My advice is to start when he is about ten years of age. He is then full of boyish spirits and eager to learn. My children started earlier, and most of them have given public displays when only four years of age.

By means of the instruction given in this book, fathers can quite easily give their boys their first lessons in boxing at home. It is a splendid method of keeping fit for both parent and sons, and there would be less need for the family doctor.

KIT.

A very sensible present for a boy is a set of boxing gloves. Be sure to get good ones, and they will last a lifetime with care.

I recommend the 6 oz. "Perfection" glove (made by Spencer, Heath and George, Goswell Road, London), as they are well padded, supple, and it is easy to clench the fist when landing a blow. My own children have been boxing since the time when they were very young, and never yet has one of them had a marked face.

After use, the gloves should be wiped well and hung up in a dry room.

PLAY-ROOM.

Friends have often said to me "You are lucky to have so clever a family, but, of course, you had the advantage of the use of army gymnasia." My family of four boys and a girl, however, has never used a gymnasium. The front living room in the quarters has been our work-room. "Clear deck" is the order, and out go the table, chairs, sofa, mats, etc. In this room my family has been taught Boxing, Acrobatic Feats, Hand-to-Hand Balancing, Dancing, Skipping, Club-Swinging, Slack Wire Walking, Games, and Physical Exercises.

Married quarters in barracks are never very spacious, so what has been possible in my case is possible in the average British home. Whenever possible, boxing and athletic exercises generally should be taken in the open air.

ON GUARD.

Left foot advanced and flat on the ground with the toe pointing towards the opponent, distance from heel to heel about 16 or 18 inches. The weight of the body resting on the left foot and the ball of the right, the latter at an angle of about 90 degrees.

The knees slightly bent, body turned to the right and inclined slightly forward. The arms raised with the left hand about as high, and in line with, the nipple of the left breast, and slightly bent, the right arm bent and close to the side with the forearm protecting the mark. The thumbs of both hands uppermost, fingers slightly bent, the left shoulder slightly raised to protect the point. The head forward and slightly lowered with the eyes fixed on the opponent.

The whole position should be one of perfect freedom and readiness of movement.

SPARRING, OR "ON GUARD" WITH ACTION OF THE ARMS.

The left arm should work by a small easy forward and backward circular movement, the right arm working in a similar manner, but between the Mark and Point, elbow close to the body.

THE ADVANCE.

Press off the toes of the right foot and advance the left a few inches, and immediately afterwards bring the right foot up the same distance, so that on completion of the movement the feet are in their original position.

THE RETIRE.

Step back a few inches with the right foot, followed by the left, observing the same principles as in "The Advance."

Another method of retiring is to press off the ball of the left foot and carry it back to the right, at the same time carrying the right foot to the rear, finishing in the position of "On Guard."

N.B.—In all "footwork" the legs should move with ease and freedom, and any tendency to stiffness must be avoided.

MOVING TO THE LEFT AND RIGHT.

Carry the left foot a few inches to the left, followed a similar distance by the right.

When moving to the right the right foot is moved first.

TURNING.

This is a movement used against an opponent who continually runs, or circles round, and is performed as follows :—

As the opponent circles to his right, pivot on the ball of the right foot to the left and carry the left foot in the direction of the opponent.

Following an opponent circling to his left, the movement would be reversed.

SWAYING.

This is a forward and backward movement of the body which, if properly executed, does away with a lot of unnecessary footwork. "Round arm" and "Swinging" blows can be easily avoided by "swaying" out of distance, and a return blow quickly delivered.

By pressing off the toes of the right foot and slightly bending the left knee, allow the body to sway forward, swaying backward being the reverse movement.

THE CLENCHED FIST.

At the moment of impact the fist should be tightly clenched with the thumb round the first two fingers, the wrist straight, and the back of the hand outward. The object aimed at should be struck with the face of the knuckles.

STEPPING IN.

This must vary according to circumstances. In the ordinary course it should be executed by advancing the left foot the required distance, at the same time firmly bracing up the muscles of the right leg. Should the opponent retire or sway out of distance, the stepping in, to avoid lunging, should be done by advancing the left foot, immediately followed by the right.

THE "POINT" AND "MARK."

To talk of being hit on the "Point" really means that one has received a blow on the chin, while being hit on the "Mark" signifies that a blow has been received on the body in the region of the navel, but just above it.

To hit below the navel is a foul, and is known as "hitting below the belt." In boxing, points are awarded for clean hitting with the knuckles of either hand on any part of the head, front and sides of the body above the belt. Although in this book special mention is made of the "Point" and "Mark," it is done so chiefly for instructional purposes, but blows on other parts are equally valuable, as far as points are concerned.

THE LEFT LEAD.

Step in and deliver a blow at opponent's "Point," bringing the left shoulder well forward and the weight of the body into the blow.

RIGHT HAND GUARD FOR POINT.

Raise the hand, partially closed, in front of the face, and contracting the muscles of the arm use a slight forward pressure to avoid the glove being forced on the face. Elbow kept close to the side, the force of the blow being taken on the heel and palm of the hand.

RIGHT HAND GUARD FOR MARK.

Contract the muscles of the abdomen and carry the right forearm across the Mark. Fist tightly clenched, elbow and forearm close to the body.

LEFT HAND GUARD FOR MARK.

Made as above, but with the left forearm.

LEFT FOREARM GUARD.

Raise the left arm forward and slightly outward. This guard is extremely useful against a " cross counter " or right swinging blow.

RIGHT FOREARM GUARD.

As above, but finishing with the right arm bent ready to deliver a "Right at Point."

RIGHT AT POINT.

Step in and deliver a blow at the Point. As the blow is delivered bring the right foot forward and slightly outward, leg braced up. This movement of the right foot will allow of the right shoulder being brought well forward, and also brings the weight of the body behind the blow. The body should be turned naturally and the left hand held in readiness for defence.

It is not meant to imply that this should be used as a "lead." It should invariably be preceded by a left lead or feint. This also applies to a "Right at Body."

LEFT AT MARK.

Stepping well in, deliver a short-arm blow at the Mark, the elbow bent and forearm horizontal. Head lowered and kept as much as possible behind the left shoulder.

RIGHT AT MARK.

Step in, but with the left foot a few inches to the left of the opponent's, and at the same time deliver a short-arm blow at the Mark, the right foot and shoulder being brought forward with the blow, the left hand drawn slightly backward and in readiness for defence.

FEINTING.

A Feint is a simulated attack, and is made with the object of deceiving an opponent and causing him to move his guard to the place feinted at, thus leaving another part unprotected. It is made by a quick, energetic, and slightly forward movement of the arms, body, and head, the whole being kept well under control, while the expression of the features should be such as to make an opponent believe that the feint is a genuine attack. One often hears advice given "not to answer a feint," but a feint well executed is sure to be answered.

Another object of feinting is to "draw" an opponent. For instance, on a "Left lead" an opponent continually uses a "Right cross counter." A feint should be made to draw the counter; this would be stopped by a "Left forearm guard," leaving the opponent absolutely open to be countered in turn.

DUCKING.

Ducking is a method employed to avoid a blow without guarding, and is used most successfully against an opponent who shows his intention, or against a person who has no variety of attack. "Ducking" can be done either to the right or left, the former being the safest, there being no fear of a "Counter." In the latter there is always a possibility of being countered by an opponent's right hand; therefore the left hand must always be in a position to prevent this. It is only possible to "Duck" when an opponent leads at the head, and whenever it is successfully performed a counter should always be delivered with it.

DUCK TO RIGHT AND COUNTER WITH LEFT AT POINT.

Incline the head slightly to the right and lower the body so that the blow intended for the head passes harmlessly over the left shoulder; at the same time step in and deliver blow at the Point.

DUCK TO RIGHT AND COUNTER WITH LEFT AT MARK.

Inclining the head as above and lowering the body, step *well* in and deliver a left at Mark.

DUCK TO RIGHT AND LEFT HAND UPPERCUT.

As in "Counter Left at Point." Deliver an uppercut by punching directly upward, at the same time bracing up the muscles of the legs and body; the elbow directly under the hand, the blow aimed under the chin. This is most successful against an opponent who leads with his head down.

Whenever a "Duck and Left Hand Counter" is carried out successfully it should immediately be followed with a "Right at Body."

GUARD FOR UPPERCUT.

This is formed as for "Right Hand Guard for Point," but owing to the direction in which the blow is travelling the pressure is made downwards.

DUCK TO LEFT AND RIGHT HAND CROSS COUNTER.

When opponent leads at head, step in with the left foot, simultaneously followed by the right, carrying the head and body inside the opponent's left arm, at the same time delivering a blow at the Point. The left foot should travel in the direction of the toes of the opponent's right, while the right hand should pass outside and close to the opponent's left arm. The whole art in "Countering" is the "time" at which the blow is delivered, the object being to bring the two forces together at the same time, *i.e.*, the right hand and opponent's jaw.

As already explained, the left hand should be in a position of defence.

DUCK TO LEFT AND RIGHT HAND COUNTER AT POINT.

The movements of the head, body, and legs are exactly the same as above, but the right hand travels *inside* and close to the opponent's left arm.

DUCK TO LEFT AND RIGHT HAND COUNTER AT MARK.

Stepping *well* in and lowering the head and body, deliver a short-arm blow at the Mark or any unprotected part of the body.

DUCK TO LEFT AND RIGHT HAND UPPERCUT.

Carrying out the same principles as in "Right Hand Counter at Point," punch directly upward, at the same time bracing up the muscles of the legs and body.

The blow should be delivered without any preliminary movement, coming directly from the Guard position. At the moment of impact the elbow should be bent and directly under the hand, the legs, head, body, and hand working together.

SLIPPING.

Slipping is practically Ducking, with the exception that the foot is carried *outside* the opponent's. Although it can be executed to either side, slipping to the left is not recommended, it being far too dangerous, seldom carrying one far enough away from an opponent to be of any advantage, whereas that to the right, if properly performed, takes one quite outside an opponent's guard. Slipping is best used against a strong rushing boxer, and is a most useful method of getting out of difficulties, such as when on the ropes or in a corner.

When in either of the latter cases a "slip" is made the positions invariably become altered.

Care should be taken after "slipping" to turn left about at once facing one's opponent, and whenever possible the "slip" should be followed by a counter at Point or Body.

THE SIDE STEP.

Another method exceedingly useful in avoiding a rush or when driven against the ropes.

By a sudden movement of the feet, half spring and half step, turning the body to the right; at the same time lower the head and bend the left elbow close to the side, forearm across the Mark. On completion of the movement the left foot should at once be brought to the Guard position.

HOOK HITS, LEFT AT HEAD OR BODY.

These are made with either hand at head or body.

Bending the arm at the elbow and without drawing back the hand, keep the wrist and forearm straight, step in close and deliver a blow at the right side of the chin; at the same time pivot the body to the right on the forepart of the right foot. The head should be lowered and inclined to the right, so that the jaw is protected by the left shoulder, the back of the hand uppermost and the elbow raised.

A "Hook Hit" at body should be carried out in exactly the same manner, excepting that the blow is directed at the body.

RIGHT HOOK AT HEAD OR BODY.

These are made in a similar manner to those with the left hand, excepting that the body is pivoted to the left and the left foot advanced to the left front at the same time.

DEVIATING, OR PUTTING A BLOW ASIDE.

In addition to the methods already explained, there are other ways of preventing a blow from landing on the head or body. A very effective way is that referred to above. This, in addition to stopping the blow, also has the effect of upsetting an opponent's equilibrium, leaving him in such a position that he is neither able to attack nor to defend himself. It can be performed with either hand, and is best executed from a "Left Lead at Head." Without drawing back the hand or raising the elbow, with a sharp forward and outward movement to the left, beat firmly with the palm of the right hand on the glove, wrist, or forearm of the opponent. The movement should be as small as possible and kept well under control.

To "Deviate" with the left hand, beat firmly as described above, but on the *inside* of the opponent's left arm. This can also be used to prevent a blow at Mark, but care should be taken that it is a close, forward, and outward movement to the left, as beginners are apt to make it downward and so carry the blow low.

BLOCKING.

Is a method adopted for "Breaking up an Attack," and is best used against an opponent who, by some preliminary movement, such as drawing back the hand, exposes his deliveries. As soon as this is detected, should it be the left hand, immediately place the right hand, with open glove, on the opponent's hand, thus preventing him from carrying out his intention. Should the intended blow be from his right, it can be "Blocked" by placing the palm of the left hand on his hand, arm or shoulder.

"IN-FIGHTING."

"In-Fighting," although such a useful asset to a boxer, is, curiously enough, sadly neglected. How often one sees, in a bout, the men get to close quarters and, not knowing what to do, immediately start to hold each other, this being, to them, the only way out of the difficulty.

To get into the most favourable position, one must first of all "Duck" so as to get inside an opponent's guard, and keeping the head down and the jaw protected with the left shoulder, force him backward, at the same time delivering a series of short-arm punches at the body, varied with uppercuts and hooks at chin. The blows should be combined with the movements of the body and feet so as to bring the greatest possible force into their delivery, while the arms working close to the sides will enable one to keep the inside position, or what is commonly known as "inside the guard."

LESSONS

The following lessons are drawn up to suit any number of pupils. It is not, however, advisable to have too large a class.

The class will be formed up in two ranks and numbered from right to left in "twos." The words "Open out" will then be given, when the odd numbers of the front rank will take two paces forward, and the even numbers of the rear rank two paces backward.

At the outset it will be necessary for the Instructor to give words of command for each movement, but as soon as the class shows reasonable progress a succession of movements should be made on a word of command being given.

The Instructor should now place himself in a boxing attitude in front of, and facing the class, explaining to the pupils that they are to move with him, but in the opposite direction. For instance, as the Instructor makes a succession of advances so the pupils retire in the same way, and *vice versa*. The Instructor moving to the left, pupils move to the right, and so on. This

CLASS OPENED OUT FOR LEGWORK UNDER LEADER. SUPERVISED —BY.— INSTRUCTOR

CORRECT POSITION FOR OFFENCE OR DEFENCE

can also be done by word or signal. This rule cannot always be carried out when the class is required to turn from one direction to another, the Instructor not being in a position to be seen by the pupils, so that a word of command such as "Left" or "Right" is necessary. The whole of the footwork can now be gone through without a pause, care being taken that the sparring and swaying is maintained throughout.

In the following lessons it is not intended that the pupils should be instructed by word of command. No good results could ever be obtained by such a method. The object is to teach, as far as possible, each individual to give at least a reasonable lesson.

The Instructor must first illustrate the lesson with a likely pupil, thoroughly explaining the movements of the one acting as leader, and afterwards those of the pupil. The class should be split up into pairs and placed about the room, one of each pair being told to act as leader, the Instructor moving about among them assisting and correcting wherever necessary.

In this manner the pupils are taught to use their brains, and, moreover, are gaining confidence quite unconsciously. Each should in turn act as leader. It is not advisable for the same pair to work together at each lesson.

Each lesson having been taught from the stationary position, the advance and retire should be at once added. To carry out the former, the pupils should lead and guard as usual, after which the leader breaks ground by retiring; the pupil then advances, and when within distance leads as above. For the latter the pupil leads as before, and after doing so retires; the leader then advances, and when within distance the pupil carries out his attack as before.

This is found to be an excellent method of teaching pupils' footwork, and at the same time giving them a good idea of distance.

INTRODUCTORY EXERCISES.

SKIPPING.

PRACTICE 1.—On both feet, with rope swinging forward; then with rope swinging backward.

PRACTICE 2.—Alternate feet; rope swinging forward first, later backward.

PRACTICE 3.—Rope-crossing, or any fancy skips.

MEDICINE BAG.

A small football case (or canvas bag) filled with rags to weigh about 1½ lbs. The bag should not be too heavy, the direction in putting being most essential.

PRACTICE 1.—Putting the bag forward with either hand. The left hand being generally the weaker, should be used most frequently. The bag must be put forward in exactly the same manner as a straight left or right punch is performed, the rear leg being firmly braced as the bag is put forward. The boy who is putting the bag should aim at his opponent's Point, the other catching bag as he would guard a punch at Point.

PRACTICE 2.—Putting the bag forward as before, aiming at Point or Mark.

1ST PRACTICE — MEDICINE BAG

3RD PRACTICE — MEDICINE BAG

MEDICINE BAG—*Continued*.

PRACTICE 3.—Dodging or Guarding. One boy standing between two others; the two outside boys throw the bag at the centre boy, who practices guarding, ducking, putting bag aside with either hand, or dodging. If he is hit on any part of the head or body above Mark, he is out, and the boy who hits him goes in centre. To make the practice harder, have four boys outside.

LESSON I.

FOOTWORK.

PRACTICE 1.—On Guard.
PRACTICE 2.—On Guard and Sparring.
PRACTICE 3.—On Guard and Swaying.
PRACTICE 4.—Advancing.
PRACTICE 5.—Retiring.

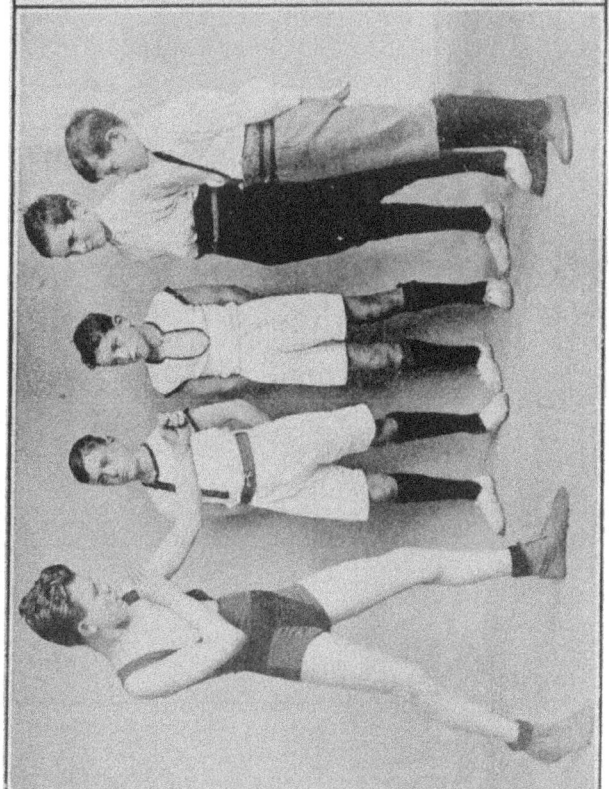

LESSON I
PRACTICE I

LEADER
DEMONSTRATING
TO CLASS
"ON GUARD"

LESSON I.—*Continued.*

PRACTICE 6.—Moving Left and Right.
PRACTICE 7.—Turning Left and Right.
PRACTICE 8.—Stepping in.

LESSON II.

LEADING AND GUARDING.

PRACTICE 1.

Pupil: Step in and left lead at Point.
Leader: Right hand guard for Point.

PRACTICE 2.

Pupil: Right hand guard for Point.
Leader: Teach right hand guard for Point.

PRACTICE 3.

Pupil: Left lead and guard Point with right.
Leader: Same as Pupil.

PRACTICE 4.

Pupil: Left and right guard for Mark.
Leader: Teach left and right guard for Mark.

LESSON III.

LEADING AND COUNTERING.

In this lesson the Leader must adapt himself to the pupil's height and reach. He must avoid "timing" any lead or counter which the pupil has to perform. In avoiding this he will find that he has to draw back the hand, a movement quite against the principles of boxing. For instance, when the pupil delivers a "Right at Point and Guards Mark with Left," the Leader, to avoid "timing" him, must draw back the left hand before delivering a blow at Mark, finishing with the arm well bent. This must be done to allow the pupil to get close enough to deliver a "Right at Point" as explained.

PRACTICE 1.

Pupil: Left lead and guard Point with right. As Leader withdraws his left, deliver a short right hand blow at Point and guard Mark with left.

Leader: Left at Point and guard Point with right. Draws hand back and delivers short arm blow at Mark, still guarding Point with right.

LESSON III—*Continued*.

PRACTICE 2.

Pupil: Left at Point and guard Mark with right. As Leader withdraws left, deliver short arm blow at Point and guard Mark with left.

Leader: Left at Mark and guard Point with right. Draw arm back and deliver short arm blow at Mark, still guarding Point with right.

LESSON III—*Continued*.

PRACTICE 3.

Pupil: Left at Mark and guard Point with right. As Leader withdraws left, deliver right at Point and guard Mark with left.

Leader: Delivers short arm blow at Point and guards Mark with right, followed by short arm blow at Mark with left, guarding Point with right.

LESSON IV.

FEINTS.

PRACTICE 1.

Pupil: Feint at Point and deliver left at Point, guarding Point with right.

Leader: Answers feint by a slight forward movement of right and then guards Point and leads with left.

PRACTICE 2.

Pupil: Feint at Mark, left at Mark, guarding Point with right.

Leader: Answers feint and guards Mark with right, delivering a short arm blow at Point.

LESSON 4 — PRACTICE 1

LESSON 4 — PRACTICE 1

LESSON IV—*Continued.*

PRACTICE 3.

Pupil: Feint at Mark and deliver left at Point, at same time guarding Point with right.

Leader: Answers feint, guards Point, and delivers left at Point at same time.

PRACTICE 4.

Pupil: Feint at Point and deliver short arm blow at Mark with left, guarding Point with right.

Leader: Answers feint and guards Mark with right, and delivers short arm blow at Point.

LESSON V.

DUCKING RIGHT AND COUNTERING WITH LEFT.

PRACTICE 1.

Leader: Left lead at Point and guard Point with right.

Pupil: Ducks Leader's lead and counters with left at Point.

PRACTICE 2.

Leader: Left lead at Point and guard Mark with right.

Pupil: Ducks and counters with left at Mark.

LESSON 5 _ PRACTICE 1

LESSON 5 _ PRACTICE 2

LESSON V—*Continued*.

PRACTICE 3.

Leader : As before, but forms guard for uppercut.

Pupil : Ducks and delivers left hand uppercut.

PRACTICE 4.

As already explained, a successful duck and counter with left should be immediately followed by right at body. The Instructor should therefore guard this blow.

LESSON VI.

DUCKING LEFT AND COUNTERING WITH RIGHT.

PRACTICE 1.

Leader: Left lead at Point and guard Point with right.

Pupil: Ducks Leader's lead and delivers right hand cross counter.

PRACTICE 2.

Leader: As above.

Pupil: Ducks and delivers right hand counter at Point.

LEADER   PUPIL

LESSON 6 — PRACTICE 1

LEADER   PUPIL

LESSON 6 — PRACTICE 2

LESSON VI—*Continued*.

PRACTICE 3.

Leader: Left lead at Point and guard Mark with right.

Pupil: Ducks and delivers right hand counter at Body.

PRACTICE 4.

Leader: As above, but forming guard for uppercut.

Pupil: Ducks and delivers right hand uppercut.

LESSON VII.

SLIPPING AND COUNTERING WITH LEFT.

PRACTICE 1.

Leader: Left lead at Point and guards Point with right.
Pupil: Slips and counters with left at Point.

PRACTICE 2.

Leader: As above, but guarding Mark with right.
Pupil: Slips and counters with left at Mark.

PRACTICE 3.

Leader: Leads as above, forming guard for uppercut.
Pupil: Slips and counters with left hand uppercut.

The pupil should now be taught to " Feint " in order to " draw " a lead, the Leader leading as an answer to the feint, the pupil ducking or slipping with a counter as explained in Lessons V, VI and VII.

LESSON VIII.

Side Step, Forearm Guards, Hook Hits, Deviating, Blocking.

The pupil, having received a good grounding in the foregoing lessons, should now be practised in the following :—

PRACTICE 1.

SIDE STEP.—Leader places pupil against a wall or rope, and, delivering a left lead, teaches the pupil side-stepping.

PRACTICE 2.

FOREARM GUARDS.—These should be taught by the Leader leading first with the left and afterwards with the right.

PRACTICE 3.

HOOK HITS.—Leader leads with left, teaches the pupil to step well in, delivering hooks with left and right at Point or Mark, Leader guarding.

LESSON VIII—*Continued.*

PRACTICE 4.

DEVIATING.—Leader leads with left, pupil deviating blow as explained.

PRACTICE 5.

BLOCKING.—Leader, making some preliminary movement with either hand, teaches the pupil how to "block" the intended attack.

The method of executing the above movements will be found under their respective headings.

NOTES ON CONDUCTING "LOOSE PLAY."

It is not advisable to commence this too soon, as beginners are very apt to acquire bad habits quickly, such as flicking with the open gloves, closing the eyes, faulty guarding, crossing the legs, etc.

The Instructor should be careful, especially in the early stages, in selecting the boys to box together, pairing them off, as near as possible, according to weight and ability, taking pains not to pair a bad performer with a good one, as nothing is more disheartening to a beginner than to be continually hit without being able to give something in return.

He must at all times keep loose play well under control, and never allow it to develop into a scramble.

Regimental Sergt.-Major E. B. Dent.

www.ingramcontent.com/pod-product-compliance
Lightning Source LLC
Chambersburg PA
CBHW060215050426
42446CB00013B/3078